THE FACE OF JESUS

ENCOUNTER HIS PRESENCE

Bryant Borges

Sid R.,

WITH GREAT HONOR AND LOVE I
BLESS YOU WITH THIS PIECE OF MY
HEART.

" TO KNOW HIM IS LIFE ETERNAL. "

The Face of Jesus: Encounter His Presence

Copyright © 2018 Bryant Borges

Cover image licensed **with permission** from Igniter Media.

i g n i t e r m e d i a . c o m

ISBN: 1717430805
ISBN-13: 978-1717430809
LOC Control Number: 2018942559

Pulpit to Page Publishing Co. books may be ordered through booksellers or by contacting:

Pulpit to Page Publishing Co.

Warsaw, Indiana

pulpittopage.com

For more information on the ministry of Bryant and
Natalie Borges visit:

THEFACEOFJESUS.ORG

DEDICATION

I dedicate this book, first and foremost, to the precious Person of Jesus Christ who intimately fastens me into Himself.

Next, I want to honor my wife for encouraging me, supporting me and interceding for me during extended periods of time with the Lord. Without her, I couldn't have fully accomplished this book in its entirety.

I lastly dedicate this book to the Church — to stir up a hunger and thirst for more of His Presence where intimacy with Jesus remains the highest priority in life. Let our cups overflow and let our communities drink of His Presence wherever we go.

A NOTE FROM THE AUTHOR

This book was inspired by various encounters and intimate visions of Jesus Christ which deepened my affection for Him. This book is meant to stir our souls to the reality of the Person of Jesus with emphasis on His Presence and His face. It is to bring hunger and a craving for more of His essence in our lives; not for merely incorporating Him into our lives but making Him the center of our existence. From Genesis to Revelation, we see that there are glorious facets to the face of God which His beloved Son carried on the earth. This book is only an introduction to encountering the manifest Presence of God by meditating on the divine Scriptures and yielding to sanctified images of Jesus' face, conceived by the Holy Spirit, revealing the eternal expression of love.

I pray that this book may be the beginning of encountering more of His Presence and cultivating a life of closeness with His Person where His habitation is your constant state of reality. I pray that this may be a tool and a testament that causes your heart to yearn for more of Jesus in the divine experiential manner where direct contact with Him becomes the common way of your transformation into His likeness. His loving face is how we encounter His Presence; to see and perceive is the beginning of knowing and beholding.

ENDORSEMENTS

"As long as I have known Bryant, his heart has been bursting with desire for the face of Jesus. This book is an overflow of what he himself has experienced. I recommend diving headlong into this work. May your heart be captivated by His beautiful face as you read."

—Eric W. Gilmour, Evangelist and Founder, Sonship International and Author of *Burn: Melting into the image of Jesus*

"I remember when I was introduced to Guyon and Fenelon. They spoke of a passion and intimacy that fanned a flame of hunger in my own heart to know this God they spoke of. In every century God has His Guyon's and Fenelon's who speak of the mystery and beauty of intimacy with God. *The Face of Jesus* is aflame with this passionate pursuit.

I have ministered alongside Bryant Borges in Brazil. I looked into the eyes of a young man wholly given in worship and service to the Face of the One he loves. In these few pages Bryant Borges takes us on the breathtaking journey from introductions to full immersion without ever losing sight of what is most important, God Himself."

—Dr. Kim Maas, Founder and C.E.O. of Kim Maas Ministries and Founder and Director of Women of Our Time (WOOT)

"I recommend reading this slowly like you would for a rich teaching by Bill Johnson or E.W. Kenyon. You don't want to miss a thing! *The Face of Jesus* is an excellent book and makes a great daily devotional."

—Brad Allen, Senior Pastor, Victory International Church

"Bryant Borges is a man hungry for the Presence of God. I first met Bryant on the mission field. His book gives a beautiful portrayal of just how brutally simple God's love is for us. No conditions, no demands, no codependent bias, at least not from His side.

And if we ever questioned His goodness as a reflection of what has happened in our own lives, then we fall short of all there is to offer in the passion of what was given to us in the scripture thousands of years ago. Bryant Borges has written pages dedicated to understanding just how passionate God's love is for us and as you unwind in each page, may these word not be another set of ideas that resolve some more theology, but may they be words that soak right into the very soul of the matter. May they heal wounds that tried to logistically fathom His kindness.

This book is a beautiful companion for times in the secret place, times to look at His perspective on whatever you may be facing right now. In reading Bryant's grace filled words you will be inspired and challenged with a powerful perspective on the nature and goodness of God. To finally understand our identity based on how He loves us, and what better way to discover that, than looking in *The Face of Jesus* and encounter His presence."

—Rev. Deborah Williams, International Evangelist and conference Speaker, Author and Founder of *Under His Wings*
Sydney, New South Wales,
Australia

"In the comments early in the book, Bryant writes that he hopes upon reading this that we would 'yearn for more of Jesus in the divine experiential manner where direct contact with Him becomes the common way of your transformation into His likeness.'

Without reservation I can say that reading this book has increased my desire to be intimate with the Lord in Worship! Moses desired to see the face of the Lord but could only handle a small portion of His back. That we would see His Glory! How my heart yearns to see His face!

—**Wayne Tate,** Site Pastor, Cliffdale Manna Church. Author, *The Worship Book*

"In language beautiful and striking, and with insightful wisdom, Brant Borges joins the long line of Christian mystics who have found inspiration and grounding in the contemplation of the face of Jesus. This book is a sound introduction to an authentic Christ-centered spirituality for new believers and has the depth to inspire the sagging spirits of the more seasoned pilgrim. No matter where you are in your faith journey, this book will encourage and stimulate you on the way to a closer friendship with Jesus."

—**Fr. Eric Ayers,** Pastor, Church of the Holy Family Catholic Church
Virginia Beach, Virginia

This book is full of life. Each page is bursting with the fire of revelation ignited from Bryant's personal encounter with Jesus. This book will cause you to long for more of Jesus and return to the simplicity of passionate devotion to the Lord. If you need fresh fuel for your pursuit of God then the *Face of Jesus* is the book for you.

—**David Fritch,** Director at *Burn 24/7*. Author of *Enthroned: Bringing God's Kingdom to Earth through Unceasing Worship and Prayer*

CONTENTS

INTRODUCTION

The end goal of this work is for you to shift your gaze from the book to His face. Christianity isn't comprised of our accrual of knowledge or our collected information where we then fulfill what's commanded with human effort. Christianity is being a laid-down lover. It is the constant pursuit of His presence. Looking at Him and depending on Him and His *paniym* or *face* is life itself. His *face* points to His *presence.* In Hebrew, **paniym** means *the face* which is used in a great variety of applications. In this context, similar to Genesis 3:8 and Exodus 33:14, the face points to His presence and countenance. When a lover yearns to see his or her beloved, all that person wants to do is be in constant contact and intimacy — face to face. Learning to live surrendered and yielded to the Holy Spirit helps us see what Jesus is doing and where He is going in the moment. Love is lived in the moment and yearned for every second.

The beauty of a life filled with bliss and love for Jesus is that the lover daily and effortlessly hosts God's presence. The lover carries the perfume of the One he walks with and spends time with. The lover lives with an awareness of His presence and walks with his heart turned to Him at all costs. This becomes the distinguishing mark of the lover. God's expression and character becomes the nature of that man/woman. Those who walk with Him treasure His face—His presence. His face is the delight and pursuit of our hearts.

As you enjoy this book on the face of Jesus, I encourage you to take pauses and moments to turn your heart to the Holy Spirit. The Holy Spirit is in love with and committed to revealing Jesus. This is His purpose and He is excited in revealing Jesus to the world. John 16:13 says, "...He will guide you into all truth. He will not speak on his own; he will speak only what he hears..." If you yield to His Presence, He will reveal Jesus to you through these pages, as it came from the holy Scriptures containing His heart for us and the world. He only asks one thing: *yield*. You won't be merely reading a book to acquire knowledge or check off another title on your list of academic accomplishments. Instead, you'll be experiencing the living God who made you to intimately experience Him. You'll begin to live the life you were made to live, within His Presence. This is

The Face of Jesus...

CHAPTER ONE

AN INTIMATE
FOCUS

"Here's the one thing I crave from God, the one
thing I seek above all else: I want the privilege of
living with him every moment in his house, finding
the sweet loveliness of his face, filled with awe,
delighting in his glory and grace."
—*Psalm 27:4 (TPT)*

In this life, there is only *one* objective. It's not ministry, service, or even work. It's not to build, create, or establish and it's not even to subdue or multiply. There is something far greater. Someone which all these beautiful realities point to. The entirety of the Scriptures simply could not be fulfilled without this absolute fact. Going further,

Jesus could not have done what He did in the gospels if this one thing did not take place daily.

What is this *one thing*? It's simple… to behold His face, to sit and stare at the person of Jesus. In it is everything one will ever need and it is why we exist. To love and be captivated by an eternal beauty that never ceases to strike awe and glory. As this essential application of love is practiced, lingering upon Jesus and all He is, it opens the soul's receptivity. It's allowing the Holy Spirit to take both spontaneous encounter and/or our imagination and bring us to gaze upon His beauty.

For instance, imagine His expression as a man, yet being God, looking at those around Him. Or what about His face as He compassionately turned to Bartimaeus and heard his cry: "Jesus, Son of David have mercy on me!" Think of Him looking at John and Mary as He was nailed to the tree. Consider Him looking at you before you were formed in the womb. This *one thing* is to sit with Him, behold Him, and to dwell on His face. It is to dine with Him at the table that He has prepared before us, even in the presence of our enemies.

Something divine happens when we have met our Love and our Lover has met us as we are known. Without receiving Love Himself, we cannot love. It is only then that we can love our neighbor as ourselves. There is only one true authentic love and He is a Person, not a verb. His name is God. God is expressed in the earth through His Son Jesus.

"

There is only one true, authentic love and it's a

Person, not a verb. His name is God.

The Scriptures say that "the Son is the radiance of God's glory." (Hebrews 1:3) Without staring at the glory of the Father which is found in the face of the Son, one simply cannot live. The Word relates, "Whoever has the Son has life; whoever does not have the Son of God does not have life." (1 John 5:12) The life source is actually not a source, it's a Person. The source of life is found in the Person of Jesus.

"But whoever is united with the Lord is one with him in spirit." (1 Corinthians 6:17) This is a divine unity that takes place. We are not to have distance from God. No, we are the house of His presence. We are the place in which His deity dwells. We are the living and breathing holy of holies. It isn't a matter of just sitting and listening to what God has to say; it's sitting and receiving the impact of His heart beating within our chest.

When we speak, it's His breath in our lungs. When we see, it's with His eyes. Even when we greet someone, it's with eyes of love, because Love intimately dwells within us. Paul declares, "I have been crucified with Christ and I no longer live, but Christ lives in me." (Galatians 2:20) If we are in Christ, purchased and saved, we no longer have the legal right to live according to our own flesh's agenda. That was crucified. We belong to our Lover and our Lover belongs to us. The Bible says, "You say, 'Food for the stomach and the stomach for food, and God will destroy them both.'" The same verse goes on to say, "but for the Lord, and the Lord for the body." (1 Corinthians 6:13) Our bodies are to be ruled and reigned by the Spirit of God. We are to yield to the eternal truth of His loving presence and put to death that which is in conflict with His Holy Spirit solely by the power of His Spirit.

The Scriptures discuss how God anoints His people and sets them apart for *only* Him. The biggest lie of the enemy is that one has been anointed for the *works* of the Lord. God hasn't anointed you merely for *works*, but for Himself. He has designed you to carry the smearing of His divine presence, the oil that runs down the locks of His hair. This isn't about ministry. This isn't about works. This is about eternity, and our eternal state begins at the cross. Our salvation is not where the journey stops… it's where it begins. Jesus came to redeem His bride back to Himself. This is why rebirth, by the Spirit, is the only way to intimately know Him. We connect by the Spirit. It is by the Spirit and in the Spirit we have eternal contact with Him, the way that is pleasurable to Him — in turn, it is ecstasy for us.

In this intimate exchange, there really isn't any separation any more. This is where you not only experience bliss but share in His sufferings. The One who has risen and ascended to the Father has a smile on His face and tears running down His eyes. He is laughing, *and* He is in agony. He is full of joy *yet* also interceding and crying out "Abba." When someone is sick and dying, the Lord grieves, and when someone experiences victory the Lord shares in it also. "Rejoice with those who rejoice; mourn with those who mourn." (Romans 12:15) Don't you know that the Lord does not exempt Himself from this reality? We are one and eternally united. What He feels I also feel. As you carry His image, His Spirit and His power, you become an offense to the plans of Satan and those blinded by the schemes of the enemy. This is because of the union we have in Christ Jesus. Nevertheless, persecution isn't a question but a promise. Jesus says in Matthew 10:22, "You will be hated by everyone because of me..." This external reality doesn't change your internal reality which is of eternal value.

Remember what Jesus said to Saul before He switched his identity to Paul: "Saul, Saul, why do you persecute me?" (Acts 9:4) Notice, Saul was heavily persecuting the church, yet Jesus took it personally and said, "why do you persecute *me*?" There is no separation between the Lord and His church in this sense. We are one body. The only severing that can take place is when the body of Christ is no longer perceiving the reality of the connection between the spirit of man and the Spirit of God. The one whom the Father has chosen can never be separated from Him. Even if His lovers wander off, He relentlessly pursues them because He is true to His covenant made by the blood of His Son Jesus (See Romans 8:39). Remember, there is no terrible sin that exists that cannot be repented of and drenched by the redemptive blood of Jesus. There is no thought too horrible, no act too violent, no sickness too great, and no sickness too small — the blood of Jesus takes it all. From a paper cut to cancer and everything in between, the blood absolves it all.

"

From a paper cut to cancer and everything in between, the blood absolves it all.

If I may be honest, The reality that my mind races as I receive His love is evidence alone that proves I desperately depend on Him. It's restlessness. Though my mind doesn't know it, my intellect and rationale cannot comprehend that Jesus paid it all. Therefore, I must submit and have my mind renewed everyday! During my love exchanges with Jesus, I surrender to the bliss of His love. This is the best way to yield—just receive, drink, and don't think.

During my love exchange with Jesus, I surrender to the bliss of His love. My soul may often wander but it is quickly found by Him. He is my soul's utmost satisfaction and nothing else will do, for "I have found the One my soul longs for." (Song of Songs 3:4)

Jesus leaves the 99 and approaches me in the midst of my restlessness and gently whispers to my heart, saying, "Come away with me — I will take you to the path of still waters. I will restore your soul."

In this moment, I respond with repentance and adoration — finding myself intimately reunited with affection by Him once again. My spirit and the Holy Spirit dance to the melody of freedom, where I am freely loving Him with all my heart. My spirit and the Holy Spirit come together. This kind of love isn't a power or an energy. It isn't something you experience one moment, and it leaves you the next. Love is a Person you talk to and walk with. It's the food that you eat which comes from His lips. We are to consume Him every second of our lives, being perpetual recipients of His love. My degenerative state comes when I stop delighting in eating, drinking and staring.

It is important to remember that we cannot do ministry nor develop work for the Lord until we receive His essence and the substance that is His presence. Our focus should not be divided but fixed on the nature of Jesus, His love for us, and His manifest

Presence dwelling in and upon us. Without this, we succumb to the things that we once were freed from. Our permanent fixation upon His face is the one ruling activity that takes precedence over all things, always.

CHAPTER TWO

THE FEAR OF THE
LORD

"Then Moses said to him, "If your Presence does not go with us, do not send us up from here."
—Exodus 33:15 (NIV)

There are many facets to the face of Jesus. In fact, Moses said to the Lord, "If your Presence does not go with us, do not send us up from here." (Exodus 33:15) The word presence here is the Hebrew word *paniym* which points to the multi-faceted face of God and literally means *face*. God, in all of His splendor and glory, cannot be captured by sight with only a pair of human eyes. Two eyes are simply not enough to capture His glory. The glory of

God is so vast that the living creatures in Ezekiel 10:2 did not just have one set of eyes. This scripture states that, "their hands and their wings, were completely full of eyes, as were their four wheels." Their multiple eyes were in full view of the glory of God, whereas man would surely die at the sight of the glorious face of God (see Exodus 33:20).

Moses understood how great God is and knew that He could not answer to the call that God gave Him without God Himself going with Him. Often times, we receive a Word from the Lord and run with it, when in reality, the Holy Spirit tests the condition of our hearts through it. Will we take His Word and run off to only report back to Him what took place... or do we live in such closeness with Him that we revere His Word, saying, "I can only go if you go with me." Moses recognized he needed God's all-encompassing nature to be present with him.

As a face contains the nature and expression of a human-being, so is the Presence of God that contains the nature and dominion of God. Wherever He goes His realm follows. The fear of the Lord is the realization that one cannot do anything apart from Him. It is the fear of knowing that if God were not present we are literally dead, hopeless, and inept. No work from human hands contain eternal value, no matter the Christian stamp of approval found on the back of it. If it isn't done in and through His Presence, it is all in vain. We need to be led by His breath. We are incomplete and severely lacking without His presence. To recognize this is the beginning of wisdom which is: the fear of the Lord.

In the multi-faceted expression of His face we see that one of the manifestations of His presence is a *holy fear*. Living in light of His holiness, we see His love being spilled over us as the blood of Jesus Christ constantly washes us — bringing us to become one with Him. It's not a fear that prohibits you from loving Him. It's not a fear that prohibits you from approaching Him with boldness. It's not a fear that paralyzes you at the sight of His face, though that happens across the Scriptures. It's a fear that causes you to recognize His Lordship and His endless love for you. It's a fear that causes you to recognize His worthiness. You can actually find delight in the fear of the Lord. The weight, burden, demand, and responsibilities of this life begin to slip off when you fear God. He is the one who lifts the burdens.

This fear also causes us to see that God doesn't need us because He lacks something, instead this was His plan since the foundation of the universe. He doesn't need us to go to the nations and evangelize because He can't do it Himself. He chooses us to go with Him and invites us to take the privileged seat and watch His awesome wonder manifest healing, salvation, and deliverance. It's His pleasure to use us. With the revelation of His heart we are to revere Him and cooperate with how He operates — not by demand but by childlike excitement awaiting to see what He is going to do next! God is eternal and we will never stop being amazed by Him — there is always something new to see.

It's our greatest privilege to be in His inner chamber of intimacy, to be the temple of His Spirit, and to host Him wherever we go. The fear of the Lord is a way of life blooming from the revelation of His holiness. He is the supreme deity and there is none like Him. The fear of the Lord is not just knowledge... *that* alone will not lead you to walk with holy reverence. It is His living presence within you transforming you and burning away every unholy thing — where He sits enthroned in the seat of your heart, where He belongs.

In Exodus 19:18, we see the Israelites at the base of Mount Sinai where thunder and smoke came with a violent tremor. God gave specific instructions to Moses that no one, not even an animal, was to approach the base of the mountain. Had they approached the mountain, they would be struck dead. This information wasn't just knowledge but it revealed God's holiness. When God came down upon the holy mountain, the Israelites said to Moses in Exodus 20:19, "Speak to us yourself and we will listen. But do not have God speak to us or we will die." Knowledge became a direct experience that affected their sinful hearts. God's heart was for them, but their hearts were far from Him. They recognized the God of miracles but didn't recognize the God of covenant. They saw

His hands but did not know His face. They had a fear of the Lord that was a literal weight upon their souls not knowing that they'd come to know the covenantal heart of God in the wilderness. While our perspective toward God tends to sway from this truth, Jesus made it possible to live from this place of covenant by His — Holy Spirit.

"

They recognized the God of miracles but didn't recognize the God of covenant.

I remember once being in the prayer closet exploring the depths of intimacy with the Holy Spirit. He continuously revealed to me the beauty of Jesus and His face. This deep hunger was a gracious invitation from Jesus Himself. I didn't know where to begin but I knew the Bible was my starting place. I finally grasped the truth — that the Bible wasn't just a historical compilation of spiritual books but manuscripts breathed by the Holy Spirit. It became like a pop-up book and it drew me in. With every passage I read, my spirit became full. What was interesting to me was that He never left me hungry but always had me craving for more. The Word became food to me, honey to my lips, and wine to my soul. As Holy Spirit romanced me into the heart and face of Jesus, I was fully captivated.

As I began to eat and drink of Him, fountains of intimacy began to spring up in my heart. During one of these intimate moments, my prayer closet shifted and the atmosphere changed completely. No longer was I surrounded by a wall of clothes and boxes of shoes. I was able to perceive His holiness like I had never imagined before. I felt so small. I wasn't familiar with such a holy presence. In this moment, He arrived in such an unexpected way as I began to softly sing to Him on my knees, just lingering upon the thought of Jesus. This is the best way I can describe it — a heavy weight struck and filled the closet. I was gripped with much awareness that He was holy and I was a sinner. In that moment I accepted that I could die off and whither just like the wind blows on the wildflowers upon the grass in season. He is a mighty God and the El Shaddai, and I am extremely fragile.

The Holy Spirit was introducing me to the fear of God and His holiness. I was closer to the carpet floor than ever. In the midst of this now paralyzing moment, I gently whispered "Jesus" and immediately felt His embrace. Despite feeling like a dirty rag and afraid of the fact that all my sins were laid bare before me, He encountered me and filled me with His holiness. Amongst many other details that I have decided to leave out, I was in awe at His majesty and grandeur. Think of the humility it takes for Almighty God to lay His glorious eyes on me (and you) and see His beloved Jesus. What was the Lord doing? There in that moment, I began to learn an aspect to His face and what the fear of the Lord was all about.

The fear of God must be an understanding that He is absolutely, unwaveringly holy. In His holiness He has His way. His Spirit is called Holy. When His Holy Spirit comes, He begins to cleanse and sanctify us. In that encounter in that closet, though I wasn't able to see His face, I felt His face upon me and His presence washed over me. I felt as though if I were to move I would be pressed down by heaviness and glory — it made me want to be ever so still.

"

The fear of God must be an understanding that He is absolutely, unwaveringly holy. In His holiness He has His way.

The fear of the Lord is the beginning of wisdom because your knowledge and understanding becomes a tangible quality of who you are. This facet of the face of God is to be cherished and respected. It changes the way you approach Him. It is with confidence and boldness, not in yourself, but in the precious Lamb of God. You cannot take the credit from the Son by any means. If we begin to walk in a manner where we emphasize our works towards holiness, this insults the Holy Spirit and His holy work in our lives. We should always give glory to the Holy Spirit at all times. This humble practice shows purity and is clear evidence that He is in our lives, working and melting us into the face of Jesus. Anything different from this is what I would call *glory-theft* and it certainly doesn't please the Holy Spirit. This is what grieving the Father looks like. If there is a day in which one does not consciously sin, one should not take credit for such living. This purity is clear evidence that He is in your life, working and moving.

You no longer worship by stumbling into a moment with God but worship with intentionality. Not entering His presence in the abundance of words but entering with a heart that reveres. It's posturing yourself before His presence with humility. God receives worship that is conceived by Him. He takes worship that He Himself motivated. It's praise and adoration that is done in the holy fear of God, not inspired by any other motives. I have no quality within myself that He desires except for that which he has conceived and birthed within me.

The fear of the Lord is one of the keys that causes us to walk in a manner that is similar to what has been written about in times past within the tabernacle of God. The outer courts were a place of sacrifice. The inner courts were a place of worship. The holy of holies was a place of holy fear. Isaiah 11:3 says, "...and he will delight in the fear of the Lord." Today, encounter the holy fear of the Lord and let it be your greatest delight. For in the outer courts, you find Jesus as your Savior, in the inner court you find the Holy

Spirit who brings the bread of the Presence and the 7 folds to His Person found in the 7-head lamp stand, and in the Holy of Holies, you come before God as your Glorious King.

CHAPTER THREE

THE FACE OF SUFFERING

"He was despised and rejected by mankind, a man of suffering, and familiar with pain. Like one from whom people hide their faces he was despised, and we held him in low esteem."
—Isaiah 53:3 (NIV)

There is another facet to the face of Jesus that the Holy Spirit has been gradually revealing to me. Some would call it a mystical encounter. Others might call it a vision, or even a thought. I choose to call it a revelation as the Holy Spirit is revealing to me vivid images and aspects of the nature of Jesus Christ —

specifically His heart. There is only one thing on the mind of the Holy Spirit and that is revealing the secrets of the Father to His people. The Scripture says, "The Spirit searches all things, even the deep things of God." (1 Corinthians 2:10) The Holy Spirit revealed to me moments of suffering, in Jesus' earthly life, that I was not aware of.

The account of Christ's sufferings can be read in Matthew 26-27 amongst other places in the gospels. While I was meditating on these Scriptures, I noticed Mary, the mother of Jesus, carrying something intimate and unique which, I believe, points to a glorious love that we as the Church are invited to have for Jesus.

Mary was Jesus' earthly mother, and though His face was completely disfigured, I'm sure she still recognized Him on the cross. After all, she birthed Him — She *knew* Him. No matter His anguished body, she recognized Him. Mary saw His feet at eye-level, as He was elevated by the cross He was nailed upon. There she was, like I'm sure she'd been many other times, at the feet of Jesus.

I once heard someone say, "His feet speak." In other words, to the one who lives at the feet of Jesus in constant adoration, that lover of Jesus finds everything he or she ever needs.

I learned in that moment of meditation that when we are unable to recognize Jesus in the midst of affliction and suffering, we need only to adore Him and we quickly find Him. His feet are the pathways into His heart.

As we simply lay our lives at His feet and find absolute abandonment in Him, the only person we ever want is Him. We make the life-long decision to live at one address — at the feet of Jesus.

"

> *Make the life-long decision to live at one address — at the feet of Jesus.*

In the midst of this gruesome moment where Jesus was on the cross, He had only one thing in His mind, you and me. He was consumed with pain but also with Love. Only Jesus would be in paralyzing agony and still be loving to the murderer next to Him. If we were able to see the pupil of the eye of Jesus, as blood ran down His face, we would be able to see humanity as the apple of His eye. In His eyes I imagine the reflection of every person standing at a distance before Him, intimately indicating that this was the very thing that brought Him to die on the cross. Jesus says in Luke 23:34, "Father, forgive them, for they do not know what they are doing." Despite the torture and suffering, He set us as the joy placed before Him by which He endured the cross and took our infirmities to die that death with Him. The death of Jesus was glorious — it meant that He would never be separated from those that believe.

Jesus died for humanity so that those who would believe would be saved. He opened up the way, truth, and life unto salvation for those who simply believed! Despite His creation striking Jesus in the face, mocking Him, slapping Him, spitting at Him, and crowning Him with a crown of thorns... He still loved every single one of them. He did what He did for humanity and every member of it. Even after His own creation punched the Creator and mocked Him, slapped Him, and crowned Him with thorns... He loved. You have to understand, in the Middle East in those days the thorns they used carried a type of sap which was poisonous. When these thorns were buried into the scalp of the victim they released a poison that burned the head of them that wore it. This is a picture of sin. Sin so easily poisons those who expose themselves to it. Yet Christ took that upon Himself to redeem us from it. He carried a love in His eye for the backslider and sinner that was and is unshaken.

In this revelation I began to see this poison from the crown dripping down and entering His own eyes. The poison dripped into His eyes almost causing blindness from the burning. Again this is my own personal encounter of His sufferings, not necessarily one that you can point to a scripture for. He cried out and gave up His Spirit — and there laid His flesh upon the tree. Not one bone broken, but His heart broken for you and for me.

It's in His suffering face that we see the love of His heart. Our perspective of the gospel and the heart of God must begin to be shaped by the reality of His agony upon the cross of Calvary. His face isn't comprised of solely smiles. His face is one of suffering as well. The sufferings were taken on by Him, for the joy set before Him... and that joy is *you*.

CHAPTER FOUR

HIS FAVOR IS HIS FACE

"Who will bring us prosperity? Let the light of your face shine on us. Fill my heart with joy when their grain and new wine abound."

—Psalm 4:6-7 (NIV)

We cannot see the face of God without first seeing the face of the Son. If we don't have Jesus in our sight, we won't be able to see God. The Son is the way to the Father. He is the truth of the Father. He uttered, "No one comes to the Father except through me." (John 14:6) Jesus is the One who draws us to the Father.

As we are drawn by the Son to see how the Father sees us, we will become more unfathomably in love with Him and walk confidently in the midst of wickedness and darkness. We need to know that we are highly favored. As we see the face of God through the glorious face of His Son, we begin to see the truth about who we are and where we stand. The loving expression on His face points to how deeply in love Jesus is with us too.

The countenance of the Father is the shining glory that beams from the face of Jesus upon His church. "Arise, shine, for your light has come, and the glory of the LORD rises upon you." (Isaiah 60:1) These verses go on to say, "Nations will come to your light, and kings to the brightness of your dawn." (Isaiah 60:3) We are carriers of hope for our communities, for our nation, for the world — because the favor of God is upon us.

Our identity is found in the countenance of the Son. His face has several expressions. He is a person. He has feelings and in His facial features we see His emotions.

Let us never forget that God Himself *feels*. His light that shines on us can be displayed as joy. It intrigues the people around us. His light is an unmerited favor that shines as an evangelistic tool, calling the world around us into an intimate place with Him.

"Then you will look and be radiant, your heart will throb and swell with joy; the wealth on the seas will be brought to you, to you the riches of the nations will come." (Isaiah 60:5) I cannot imagine a life without the radiance of the Father.

His face is always turned toward us because He is pleased with us! All He sees, for those of us in Christ Jesus, is what He had imagined from the foundation of the universe. You look like everything He ever wanted and imagined. You are perfect, made in His likeness!

As a father or mother sees the beauty of their newborn child and the comparable features they carry, similarly, our Heavenly Father sees us with joy and delight as He sees His own resemblance in us. He is a loving Father.

We have access to the enjoyment of this favor by kissing the Son. Let me explain. When we value and live dependent upon the affection that the Son has for us, it begins to form our identity.

We begin to see the favor and blessing of God. It's from this place that the Holy Spirit begins to urge us to take risks and step out of the boat. See, there is no such thing as falling when you're in the arms of God.

"

We have access to the enjoyment of this favor by kissing the Son.

Failure is often misunderstood. What is failure for me might not be failure in the eyes of the Lord. The spirit of fear tends to distort our perception of the face of Jesus. As a result we won't fully walk out the favor that Jesus purchased for us. This favor breeds a confidence in our Christian walk.

The Father shifted His gaze on the cross away from Jesus. He forsook the Son. Why? So that He could eternally look to you. Jesus went without the countenance of the Father for a moment, so we'd never go without it. Never allow fear to bring you into doubt and insecurity or uncertainty. Let's look at an example in the life of Moses:

"Moses bowed to the ground at once and worshiped. 'Lord,' he said, 'if I have found favor in your eyes, then let the Lord go with us.'" (Exodus 34:8-9)

When a spirit of fear comes, it comes to challenge the reality that God is favorable toward you and that God is with you permanently. What Satan did to Jesus in the wilderness, he does to us today.

He continually seeks an opportune time to cause us to question whether or not God is with us. If he can get you to doubt the presence of God, he can get you to doubt the promises of God.

Satan challenged Jesus' identity in the wilderness repetitively. He does the same thing with us today. However, our identity is not wrapped up in our own identity or reputation... even when those things are good. Our identity is found in the greatest personality to ever cross the horizon of this world — Jesus Christ. He is supreme and eternal. Favor is experienced when we submit to His love and *believe*.

There is total freedom found when we receive Jesus' favorable countenance upon us. When the Father sees us as His children, He doesn't simply see us, He truly sees Jesus.

When we reject the Son, He looks upon us and sees a stubborn and unrighteous people. Look at the end of verse nine from the chapter we read earlier:

"Although this is a stiff-necked people, forgive our wickedness and our sin, and take us as your inheritance." (Exodus 34:9)

See, when we reject the Son, not only does it hurt the Father, but He no longer is able to see us with His attributes. To those who believe in and cling to Jesus, we quickly begin to perceive God's favor toward us — the warmth of His Presence daily becomes real to us.

The favor of God isn't simply getting the job we applied for or getting supernatural help when we lack resources. Favor is something that's higher than those simple truths. Favor is us being made into a new creation, seated in heavenly places at the right hand of God — washed clean and made new. We transition from being earthly beings to heavenly beings, dwelling in an eternal realm. When the enemy comes to remind you of your past and convince you that you have no future, simply look to heaven and remember that you dwell and operate in an eternal realm that's higher than past, present, and future. You're at the right hand of God, as a believer.

The word favor is found in the word favorite. It's a harsh truth, but we see it in the scriptures that a few disciples were closer to Jesus than others... even though all were welcome to sit and eat at the table, John had his head on the chest of Jesus.

Peter, James, and John were often invited to closer encounters with Jesus when everyone else waited. See, He loves us all greatly and uniquely yet His favor is upon those who look to Him.

He favors us and His favorite view is us. His favorite picture is us. What brings Him joy is the sight of His people covered in the blood of His Son and filled with His very own Spirit. Those who only desire Jesus, walk the closest with Jesus. For these, their singular objective is Him — as we unpacked in chapter one.

"

He favors us and His favorite view is us.

When we see that the Father favors us and we respond and interact with Him, He grants us access to deep realms. There are realms in God that *friends* have access to. Yet I believe there are deeper realms that Revelation talks about. These are bridal realms. Realms of intimacy with God that aren't only bringing emphasis on being close as *friends* but also being *ONE* with God. This is a place in God that I personally desire greatly to abide in. I pray it to become my constant awareness so that in the natural and in the spiritual, Him and I are one just like in holy matrimony. This is obtained by the yielding of His bridal pull for us — we only need to surrender. This will all be perfected when we come to the wedding banquet with Jesus our Bridegroom and finally dine in glorified bodies with Him.

The favor of God shows us that we can all be His favorites ... all are welcomed but not all will choose *to get closer*. Many beheld Christ on the cross but only some sat at the base as He was elevated on the tree. Many were at the table yet only one put his head on His chest.

See, by iteration we can make the most of the favor He has given us. One cannot go after God unless God has touched the heart to go after Him. We must yield and surrender to this touch and this drawing. If you desire to experience the favor of the Lord, I invite you to pray a simple prayer of asking, seeking, and knocking. He will touch our hearts, as we simply yield to His pull. Before you go straight into this prayer, find a quiet place, put your attention on Jesus, and be in expectation to receive a sensitivity to His Presence as you recite this prayer with an open heart. Are you ready? Let's pray:

Holy Spirit, You are Lord, You are holy, mighty and there is none like You. (Pause and let that resonate into your heart.) You are the beginning, and end. You are eternal. Because of this, I worship You. I pause and revere Your Presence. (Pause and perceive Him in the place where you are and in your heart.)

I long to have You take hold of my heart and all of its affections. Dethrone every other lord in my heart that tries to take Your place. Let Your face be all that I see. May my heart's affection be fixed upon You. (Pause)

Lovely Spirit of God, take me and wrap me into Your Presence. I receive You as my Love, Lord, and Savior. I repent of my sins and ask for a fresh baptism of love. Enable me to walk beneath the shining countenance of Your face and be fully aware of this royal truth. Take me into the depths of the face of Jesus. Show me the favor and joy found in Jesus. That I may walk in this favor and rejoice in this truth.

I receive you open heartedly. I love you and worship you. In Jesus name. Amen!

CHAPTER FIVE

WORSHIP IS

SEEING

"But when he saw Jesus afar off, he ran and
worshipped him…"
—Mark 5:6 (KJV)

"When Jesus had again crossed over by boat to the other side of the lake, a large crowd gathered around him while he was by the lake. Then one of the synagogue leaders, named Jairus, came, and when he saw Jesus, he fell at his feet." (Mark 5:21-22)

My prayer for you in this chapter is that the Holy Spirit may crack open your heart and infuse the revelation of worship which is far greater than what is written in these next few pages. Worship and adoration are the organic responses to seeing Jesus. This was what Jairus experienced. It's understood that the word worship means to lay down at one's feet. To prostrate oneself at the feet of the One being worshipped is the literal picture of the word worship.

Sometimes worship is a response birthed from a place of desperation. It not only shows humility, it demonstrates a heart dependent and eager for more of Jesus. In the gospels for example, there were moments when people saw the face of Jesus and instantly recognized His deity and worship was an automatic response. It's an irrefutable pattern in the Word. That same chapter from earlier relates, "When he saw Jesus from a distance, he ran and fell on his knees in front of him." (Mark 5:6)

The book of Revelation speaks of the worship that will take place upon our seeing Jesus in heaven. We will not only reach the peak of eternal satisfaction but it will be a continuation of worship and adoration. Worship is a spiritual activity, not an intellectual activity. Upon seeing by the Spirit (see John 4:24), we immediately perceive His beauty and adore. What's even more beautiful, is seeing our spirit permeate into our soul and our emotions becoming a holy response deeply influenced by the Holy Spirit. In Isaiah and Ezekiel, the living creatures are known to have many eyes and they never miss the glory of the Lord, for they are assigned to the chamber with God's glory. In fact the prophetic book of Revelation also speaks of these beings:

"Also in front of the throne there was what looked like a sea of glass, clear as crystal.

In the center, around the throne, were four living creatures, and **they were covered with eyes**, in front and in back.

The first living creature was like a lion, the second was like an ox, the third had a face like a man, the fourth was like a flying eagle. Each of the four living creatures had six wings and was covered **with eyes all around, even under its wings**.

Day and night, they never stop saying: "Holy, holy, holy is the Lord God Almighty, who was, and is, and is to come." Whenever the living creatures give glory, honor and thanks to him who sits on the throne and who lives for ever and ever, the **twenty-four elders fall down before him who sits on the throne** and worship him who lives for ever and ever. They lay their crowns before the throne and say: "You are worthy, our Lord and God, to receive glory and honor and power, for you created all things, and by your will they were created and have their being." (Revelation 4:6-11 emphasis added)

Notice, the creatures were covered with eyes all around. Why? Because of an absolute need to *see* the Lord. It's as if they have many eyes so that they don't miss him. Not only that, but take note of the elder's response — throwing themselves down, as well as their own crowns (accomplishments) in worship.

Sometimes, we don't quite grasp what worship itself actually looks like. Worship isn't just about listening to spiritual music or even being in a holy setting. Worship is engaging your soul with Him. Your soul is your mind, will, and emotions. Worship is focusing your gaze on His face when no one is watching. As we engage our souls with Him things change. When those moments end, we are left with a wonderful nostalgia…

remembering the moments we had with Him. Those memories draw us back to the secret place with Him and thus the cycle continues. This is how we can walk in the secret place of the Most High — by simple adoration. He beautifully draws us in.

As we go throughout our day, it is possible to position ourselves to focus (and refocus our gaze back) on Jesus. Friends, we are in holy covenant with Him, that never stops, withers or changes. The biggest hinging point is *faith*. We must believe the scriptures that declare we are indeed in union with Jesus. We must believe whole-heartedly that we are able to connect with Him. As we exercise our faith this way, His presence comes. Even as you converse with another person, you are able to remain fixated on Jesus. It isn't disrespectful but indeed a blessing to those around you when they engage with a person who is constantly beholding Jesus.

This is the means by which God changes the world. This is how kings and queens are influenced. This is how prime ministers and presidents turn and make shifts. This is how economies bounce back and communities are turned upside down in all the right ways. It happens through people like you and me maintaining a steady worshipful gaze upon His face. As we look at Jesus, people will look to us and see Jesus. It's the only place of bliss and satisfaction.

There is a practical tool that I see in the gospels that I want you to take note of:

"After saying this, he spit on the ground, made some mud with the saliva, and put it on the man's eyes. 'Go,' he told him, 'wash in the Pool of Siloam' (this word means "Sent").

So the man went, washed and came home seeing." (John 9:6-7)

I believe that as this man recovered his eye sight through the miraculous power of Jesus, the very first thing this man saw, was Jesus Himself. How precious is that? The very first thing He sees in his life, is Life itself. If you study healings in the gospels, very often Jesus requires an act of faith on the part of the person receiving their healing.

Notice, Jesus didn't simply give the man a miracle. The man had to "go and wash." We don't know how the man got to the Pool of Siloam. It probably required that he ask for directions and feel his way there. It took effort. Yet his actions were an act of faith to get what God had for him. In this same way, experiencing God requires true acts of faith. For some, they might imagine what the face of Jesus looks like as they approach Him in prayer and intimacy. This is one way; however, I believe the act of faith is something deeper.

I personally begin to meditate on scriptural text and look for Jesus in them. For instance, I have meditated on Luke 10:34 where it speaks about the Samaritan and it says, "He went to him and bandaged his wounds pouring on oil and wine." As I linger upon this text, I allow the Spirit of God to reveal to me Jesus and begin to see that *wine* is the symbol of the new covenant and *oil* is the symbol of the Spirit which He pours out after His ascension.

In seeing this, I grow deeper in love with Jesus as I focus on how He opened this divine relationship for us so that He can be intimately one with us forever — it is all by this new covenant and by His very own Spirit. I also consider how the bandage, which the Samaritan used, being the Word of God — prevents further wounds and assists in healing! This is just one example where we can see symbols of Jesus in the word. There is much He wants to reveal to us through the scriptures.

As we ruminate on who Jesus is, the way the Scriptures reveal Him to be, we are drawn to worship. We see in Isaiah 53:2 that Jesus "had no beauty or majesty to attract us to him, nothing in his appearance that we should desire him." With this in mind, I would wonder, what initially brought people to Jesus? Clearly, it was His nature, His character, His love and compassion for all. As I would go into my secret place, I would begin my time of worship by imagining that I am really meeting with Him. Then, I intentionally wait to be drawn to worship by the Holy Spirit. I would ponder on who He is and would remember all He has done. Psalm

34:1 says, "I will extol the Lord at all times; his praise will always be on my lips." David sings praises because he is reminded of God's goodness and who He is. As I practiced this, the Spirit would reveal to me all the good things He has done for me.

During these moments, I am drawn to worship and my heart overflows with love for Him. These times are very special and intimate because we really step into 1 John 4:19 where it says, "We love because He first loved us."

An image of Jesus like this is so needed in the church today. Seeing Him like this creates a worshipful auto-response within us. He becomes so easy to adore and admire when we see Him as He is. We were the joy set before Jesus and now He is the joy set before us. It's our honor and privilege to share in His sufferings and to worshipfully approach

Him in secret where His inner chambers of intimacy are made just for us.

"

We were the joy set before Jesus and now He is the joy set before us.

We are called to live interwoven in the activities of the Holy Spirit. We are to be forever intoxicated by the joy that He freely offers. We are to live in the richness of Christ where rivers of living water flow in and through us. It was because of Jesus' sufferings that the dam broke open and now rivers of glory are open to us.

This leads us to worship and is also what the Seraphim's began saying as they called to one another in the throne room of God: *The whole earth is full of His glory.* The only thing we are invited to do is have a daily fixation on Him and a steady denial of the flesh. This is the life we are called to. This is worship!

CHAPTER SIX

EYES OF FIRE

*"His eyes are like blazing fire, and on his head
are many crowns."*
—Revelation 19:12 (NIV)

There was one afternoon in which I was driving around town with my wife. I was meditating on the face of Jesus and two scriptures came to my mind as the Holy Spirit emphasized His eyes to me. Those scriptures were:

"The eye is the lamp of the body. If your eyes are healthy, your whole body will be full of light." (Matthew 6:22)

"His eyes are like blazing fire, and on his head are many crowns. He has a name written on him that no one knows but he himself." (Revelation 19:12)

As I studied Scriptures, I began to see how the Bible continually relates the eyes of Christ to eyes that illuminate – eyes of fire. I started to unpack my heart on the subject to my wife. I asked for her opinion on the matter. She is a woman who is mightily used in prayer and intercession and is wise beyond her years. She said, "Bryant, I encourage you to envision the pillar of fire that was used to illuminate the path for the Israelites in the dessert. There's so much to unpack there." She kept saying that she felt like a revelation was within that text.

A moment later a revelation came so clearly to me and it blew me away. The pillar of fire for the Israelites was their compass. They had no map or compass to guide them into Canaan. It was the splendor, beauty and glory of God that led them. The Spirit of God began to show me how in our lives, the fire of His presence must be the compass by which we navigate through life. Simply put, without His presence we are lost. As my wife challenged me to dig into this text, I saw an image in my mind's eye in which the beaming eyes of fire from Revelation 19:12 were looking upon the Israelites and as the face of God shined upon the Israelites — they followed. It was as if torches protruding from Christ's eyes became the pillar that led the Israelites.

When I realized this, it further increased my dependency on His face. I cannot go anywhere if I lose sight of His face. I can't afford to make grandiose plans without consulting the Lord in the light of His face and wait and watch what He does and says. His presence must be at the forefront. To know that His countenance is continually upon me is a responsibility that urges us to follow where He goes.

"

I can't afford to make grandiose plans without consulting His face.

Let me explain, If I am in a supermarket or on a school campus, or wherever the Lord leads me to go – I am continually watching and asking, "What is the Holy Spirit asking and doing?" If I am talking to someone, I am continually making it a habit to ask what the Spirit is doing and saying in that moment, or to that person. There was a time that I was pulling out of the gym and the Holy Spirit moved me to look to the right of my vehicle and focus. Several hundred yards away the Holy Spirit dialed my eyes in on a man who was sitting on a bench at a park with his eyes down. I immediately knew that God wanted me to approach him as a conduit for the Lord.

I drove over, approached, and simply said, "Hey man, my name is Bryant. Do you mind if I pray with you?" He looked at me with astonishment... completely bewildered. He looked up, "What?" I repeated, "Do you mind if I pray with you?" He began weeping uncontrollably. I was then able to pray for him and minister to him. It became clear that the Holy Spirit had arranged the appointment and was moving.

What happened in this story? I simply looked where Jesus looked. When we do this, when we are led by Him — God's gaze of affection is our compass toward destiny —

not only ours but it blesses and empowers the lives of the people around us. This brings Him glory and delight. In this place of devotion, we see the bride and the Groom beautifully dancing in sync. The Holy Spirit turns our gaze to Jesus and we live looking at life through His eyes. This is the manner in which He leads. Would you be willing to make it your life's ambition to simply follow the gaze of Jesus Christ?

A life that is yielded to the activity of the Spirit is the answer. It begins as a life that's dedicated to being with the Holy Spirit. Ministry by the Spirit doesn't come without intimacy with the Spirit. When you look into the scriptures you see a life of fellowship with the Spirit lived out. Paul said, "May the grace of the Lord Jesus Christ, and the love of God, and the **fellowship of the Holy Spirit be with you all**." (2 Corinthians 13:14 emphasis added)

"

Ministry by the Spirit doesn't come without intimacy with the Spirit.

Derek Prince once said, "There are two religions. One is based on works and abiding by the law. The other religion is based on grace and faith." The first religion requires you to obtain your own salvation. The second one is based on a person who has already bought your salvation. Christ paid a price that we couldn't pay, now in return we simply gaze and keep our eyes positioned on Him.

The emphasis on His eyes and following where His eyes go is one that I can't bring out enough. It's our compass and our guide.

May we match the steady gaze that He is giving us with a steady gaze in return.

"By day the Lord went ahead of them in a pillar of cloud to guide them on their way and by night in a pillar of fire to give them light, so that they could travel by day or night." (Exodus 13:21)

Growing up in church, I've heard it said many times that the wilderness is a place of loneliness and solitude in which the voice of God is no longer available. When we look at the account in Exodus — God is ever available. He is continually manifesting, leading, guiding and speaking. Spirituality is not dried up. See, as long as we are fixed on Him, we will never experience devastating disappointment. Disappointment comes when our expectations are not met. Our expectations come from what we see Him doing and we are ever so fulfilled in this.

Moreover, the Israelites never went without. Their clothes never wore out and their children's sandals were never too small. Their clothes grew with them! If we only fix our eyes on the pillar of fire projected by His eyes, everything we ever need follows.

A life lived in Him and with Him is one that is continually fulfilled. There is no room for disappointment on the agenda when our agenda is simply Him. May His eyes guide you. May your wilderness season be a season in which your spiritual compass is dialed in place by the Holy Spirit who will reveal to you *Jesus*. He will teach you to follow His eyes. Whatever season you find yourself in, I pray that as you fix your gaze on His eyes of fire, that it set ablaze the trail before you. He is the lamp to your feet and the light to your path.

CHAPTER SEVEN

THE PRIESTLY BLESSING

"The Lord bless you and keep you; the Lord make his face shine on you and be gracious to you; the Lord turn his face toward you and give you peace. So they will put my name on the Israelites, and I will bless them."
—Number 6:24-27 (NIV)

The root word for blessing is *barak,* which means to kneel by implication to bless. At the last supper, Jesus knelt down to wash the disciple's feet. This was the perfect word-picture of the Hebrew word "bless" because it demonstrates serving in humility, which is the way we are shepherded by our Lord who is our Great Shephard: YHWH-Rohi.

Having the direct translation to the Hebrew word for blessing is important in understanding a few intimate aspects of the Priestly Blessing. This blessing was given to Moses by the Lord. There is so much beauty and loveliness in this blessing. This isn't your typical "blessing." When you look at the priestly blessing — the Lord is saying, "I am your Father, and I am here to serve you... lovingly and humbly with my own life." Does the blessing state that verbatim? No, but let me reveal to you how this message is intertwined within the blessing. Let's read:

"The Lord said to Moses, 'Tell Aaron and his sons, this is how you are to bless the Israelites. Say to them: The Lord bless you and keep you; the Lord make his face shine

on you and be gracious to you; the Lord turn his face toward you and give you peace.'
So they will put my name on the Israelites, and I will bless them." (Numbers 6:23-27)

This was the blessing released to the Israelites — the nation that was under covenant with the Lord. As gentiles who were *outside* of covenant with God, this blessing was not available. When you look to the gospels in the New Covenant, however, you see the blessing given to the gentiles as well. We now have been welcomed into the priestly blessing by the shedding of Christ's blood. Gentiles in the Old Covenant would have longed to experience such a blessing but simply had no access. As gentiles in the New Covenant, we too have access to this beautiful expression from the Father. Brothers and sisters, let us not ignore the welcoming we've been granted.

In the Old Testament description of the Tabernacle, in the inner courts we see the "bread of the presence" being stationed there very specifically. The word presence means "faces or facets." In this, we now see how Heaven's Darling — Jesus, was sent to you and me that we as a people would be served well. He Himself called Himself the "bread of life." In the Tabernacle, the bread was to be fresh out of the oven and the fragrance and smoke would have mixed with the burning incense creating a specific atmosphere and aroma.

This represents Jesus, the bread of heaven, being brought into our lives as the fragrance of the Father — feeding us, serving us, and changing our atmosphere. These are the gems and delights that come with His presence. The presence of the Lord is daily consumable. As we consume Him He comes out of our pours, as it were. He becomes the substance we release all around our spheres of influence.

"

This represents Jesus, the bread of heaven, being brought into our lives as the fragrance of the Father — feeding us, serving us, and changing our atmosphere. These are the gems and delights that come with His presence.

Verse 25 of the verse above says, "and be gracious to you." Grace is the gift of God to us as sons and daughters. We aren't merely justified by the blood, but sanctified by His blood which gifts us with the empowerment of His grace. It's an integral part of the blessing that has actually been upgraded now by Christ. Grace in the Old Testament wasn't status quo or commonplace. Now, grace has been freely dispensed for all and to all.

As we continue to unpack the Priestly Blessing, we see that the Lord gave instructions to Moses in order for him to teach Aaron and his sons the manner by which they were to administrate the blessing. Jesus is now the priest and it's through Jesus that we receive the blessing. It isn't Aaron or a descendent of his who is officiating on our behalf… it's Jesus. Yet, Jesus isn't in this Old Testament passage. However, we do see

Jesus in the Old Testament by the priestly nature that Aaron and His sons carry. It's prophetic in nature because the Lord was saying to Moses that the blessing would continue to be carried out through the priestly office until Christ. Christ has now stepped into that office as our High Priest forever who doesn't offer sacrifices once per year for some, but He offered one sacrifice, one time, for *all*.

The blessing continues, "the Lord turn his face toward you and give you peace." Peace is the Hebrew word Shalom. A peace that doesn't fade and is permanently provided by the Father. These things all point to the *servanthood* of God. It all displays the desire of God to care for His children.

The priestly blessing is finalized with, "So they will put my name on the Israelites." This doesn't simply mean they will say the name of the Lord. It's something deeper and weighs much more. It means they will bear his character and represent His heart. It means they will care about what He cares about. This is the seal that we are called to! God has endeavored to seal us. Let's look at a powerful passage in the passion translation:

"Now we have been stamped with the seal of the promised Holy Spirit. He is given to us like an engagement ring is given to a bride, as the first installment of what's coming!" (Ephesians 1:13-14 TPT)

The Old Testament blessing to Israel has now become an eternal blessing to all who will receive Christ. The face of Jesus makes such things available to any who will simply look at Him and trust in His name. Jesus is the face of the Father. He is God the Father *revealed*. As we look to Him, He looks back at us with a nourishing smile. His face is

reassuring; it deeply affirms us. You are His.
He calls you His beloved child, in whom He
is well pleased.

CHAPTER EIGHT

IMPARTATION OF LOVE AND BLISS

"Let him smother me with kisses—his Spirit-kiss divine. So kind are your caresses, I drink them in like the sweetest wine!"
Song of Songs 1:2 (TPT)

To have the intellectual knowledge but no experience of the One, is to come short of the full sacrifice poured out on the cross for all humanity. By direct encounter, Jesus teaches us, disciples us, empowers us, edifies us, comforts us, laughs with us, cries with us, and vibrantly lives within us. His countenance appearing to humanity 2,000 plus years ago, in flesh, caused a shift in the human race that was unprecedented and hasn't been matched since... nor will it ever be. When His precious face appears to you, by the Spirit of God, it's impossible to remain as you are.

My desire for you is that an affection for Jesus would be cultivated... that this tool may be dry wood thrown into the fire of your soul and spirit — to burn relentlessly in love with Jesus. I hope that what you've stepped into, this intimate place of glory, urges you to never trade it for anything or any other. That His face, the face of Jesus, may be all you could ever want and forever will be all you need. That your watchful eyes and searching heart may always be yielded to what He is doing and saying. We live in this sweet privileged reality where our lives are for Him as we are the Father's gift to His Son — the Bride of Christ. Let what you've discovered urge you to stare at the face of Jesus in a new way. Be watchful of His eyes and be mindful of His gaze. Look where He is looking and let Him be your life's compass. Why? Because life apart from the face of Jesus isn't life at all.

If you long for a deeper affection for Jesus — to carry His abiding Presence and glory, you only need to ask Him and spend time with Him. There are simply no shortcuts. However, I want to pray with you and impart a gift of grace that is upon my life to have a hunger, yearning, and even the time to literally come away and be with Jesus. You may see open spaces, opportunities, and moments, where you can actually spend more time with Him than usual. The price may seem high at times, amidst everything in life, it involves denying yourself and your will *daily*, but it is well worth it. You will find yourself wanting to give more than just your time but He will whisper into your heart and say, "*All I want is you.*" Today, answer to His pull after this prayer and tangibly live in the throne-room of Love where the Father, Son and Holy Spirit fellowship. Remember, as much as we may want Him, nothing compares to how much He wants us.

Say this with me out loud and get ready to be gripped with power and love by Jesus Himself:

Father, I thank you for your precious Son Jesus. The One who gave Himself so that I may be reconciled to You. I submit to the truth that You love me more than I could ever love You. I simply cannot do what You long for me to do. Therefore, I give you my heart, my will, my affections, and I give You my life. Give me Your Holy Spirit and baptize me in Your love and fire. (Turn open the palms of your hands and now receive.) Holy Spirit come. (Pause and wait quietly.) Fill me now to the overflowing measure. (Pause) In Jesus name. Amen.

Let Him take you by the hand and lure you with His kisses. His face will forever change you. You will never be the same again.

"Let brilliant light shine out of darkness, 'is the one who has cascaded his light into us — the brilliant dawning light of the glorious knowledge of God as we gaze into **the face of Jesus Christ**.'"
—2 Corinthians 4:6 (TPT emphasis added)

Prayer for Salvation

(Intimately being reconciled back to your destined home where eternal life, love and completeness are experienced now)

Pray this out loud:

Jesus, I thank you for your death on the cross. You took my sentence to death so that I may have a sentence to live for all eternity with you in heaven. I repent of my sins and turn away from them today. I give my life to You. Be my Lord and Savior. Wash me with your blood and cleans me now. Make me new. I am yours forever. In Jesus name, amen.

If this was your first time receiving Jesus or you have recommitted your life to Jesus, I encourage you to find a local church where you can be knitted into a Jesus-loving place throughout the week. Also, grab a Bible and ask Jesus to reveal to you all truth. He will begin to speak to you about Himself and will bring you to live freely and fruitfully all the days of your life!

Welcome to the eternal life and to your new family in Jesus Christ.

ABOUT THE AUTHOR

Bryant is an honorably discharged Captain of the U.S. Army. After serving 8 years in the service, he and his family were called by the Holy Spirit, in the middle of his career, to preach the Gospel to the nations and equip the body of Christ. After a sovereign encounter with the Person of Jesus Christ and the power of the Holy Spirit, he was walking the streets sharing the Gospel, healing the sick and hosting house groups.

Bryant recently ministered with Global Awakening in Brazil and he, along with his wife Natalie and first son Levi, went to Tanzania Africa as a family, to encourage and equip missionaries while supporting their ministry on the ground. Bryant is now completing his last year at Regent University in Virginia Beach pursuing his Masters in Practical Theology and Healing. They have plans to take the Gospel to the nations and equip the body of Christ. He and his wife actively serve at Big House Church where they are closely integrated with their brothers and sisters in Christ.

THE FACE
OF JESUS

ENCOUNTER HIS
PRESENCE

Bryant Borges

pulpittopage.com

Made in the USA
Lexington, KY
01 August 2018